5.3/2.0

TANGLED HISTORY

FROM FUGITIVE TO FREEDOM

The Story of
the Underground Railroad

BY STEVEN OTFINOSKI

Consultant:
Richard Bell, PhD
Associate Professor of History
University of Maryland, College Park

CAPSTONE PRESS
a capstone imprint

Tangled History is published by Capstone Press,
1710 Roe Crest Drive, North Mankato, Minnesota 56003
www.mycapstone.com

Library of Congress Cataloging-in-Publication Data
Names: Otfinoski, Steven, author.
Title: From fugitive to freedom : the story of the underground railroad /
by Steven Otfinoski.
Description: North Mankato, Minnesota : Capstone Press, 2017. | Series:
Tangled history | Includes bibliographical references and index. | Audience:
Ages 9–14. | Audience: Grade 4 to 6.
Identifiers: LCCN 2016038585
ISBN 9781515736042 (library binding)
ISBN 9781515736080 (pbk.)
ISBN 9781515736202 (ebook (pdf)
Subjects: LCSH: Underground Railroad—Juvenile literature. | Fugitive slaves—
United States—History—19th century—Juvenile literature. | Antislavery
movements—United States—History—19th century—Juvenile literature.
Classification: LCC E450 .O84 2017 | DDC 973.7/115—dc23
LC record available at https://lccn.loc.gov/2016038585

Editorial Credits
Adrian Vigliano, editor; Kyle Grenz, designer; Tracy Cummins, media researcher;
Laura Manthe, production specialist

Photo Credits
Bridgeman Images: Frey, Matthew (b.1974)/Private Collection/Wood Ronsaville Harlin, Inc. USA, 68; flickr:
Boston Public Library, 73, Internet Archive Book Images, 85; Getty Images: Buyenlarge, 83, 99, Chicago
History Museum, 64, Corbis/VCG/Photo by Library of Congress, 7, Hulton Archive, 21, 37; Granger: 74,
Sarin Images, 63; iStockphoto: HultonArchive, 16; Library of Congress: 15, 44, 91, 92, 95, 102, 105; National
Geographic Creative: JERRY PINKNEY, 86, 101; New York Public Library: Lionel Pincus and Princess Firyal
Map Division, 60, Schomburg Center for Research in Black Culture, Photographs and Prints Division, 5,
22, 29, 32, 38, 56; North Wind Picture Archives: 52, 80; Shutterstock: Everett Historical, 8, 51, 78, Nadezda
Razvodovska, Cover Design Element, Olivier Le Queinec, Cover Inset; Thinkstock: Photos.com, Cover;
Wikimedia: Public Domain, 4, Scenes in the Life of Harriet Tubman by Sarah H Bradford, 24

Printed in the United States of America.
10063S17

TABLE OF
CONTENTS

Foreword... 4

1 Slaves and Masters 8

2 The Cost of Freedom.. 16

3 A Shock to the System 22

4 Escape Plans 32

5 The Journey Begins.. 38

6 On the Run.. 44

7 The Price of Freedom 52

8 The Bridge 64

9 A Block in the Road... 68

10 A New Plan.. 74

11 Dangerous Crossing... 78

12 The Final Push.. 86

13 Free at Last.. 92

Epilogue 100

Timeline... 106

Glossary 108

Critical Thinking Using the Common Core............. 109

Internet Sites 109

Further Reading... 110

Selected Bibliography... 111

Index.. 112

About the Author 112

FOREWORD

Enslaved black people in the Americas had been risking their lives trying to escape their bonds almost since the first African slaves arrived in Jamestown, Virginia, in 1619. And for many years there were people opposed to slavery who were willing to help these people in their journey to freedom. By the 1840s, a system of safe houses had developed in the United States where fugitive slaves from the South could be hidden and protected on their journey north to free states. This secret network came to be called the Underground Railroad. Although it was neither underground nor a railroad, its members borrowed the language of train travel. Those working on the railroad were "agents." Some agents were "conductors," who guided their "cargo" of fugitive slaves, from "station" to "station." The safe houses were owned or operated by other agents, who were called "stationmasters." The final destination of most fugitives was the relative safety of northern states, where slavery had been banned. Some would travel farther north to the greater safety of Canada.

Enslaved people escaped by foot or any other type of transportation available.

Among the many fugitive slaves who reached freedom in this period was a determined young woman named Harriet Tubman. In September 1849, she left her husband and family in Dorchester County, Maryland, and fled north, probably with the assistance of agents on the Underground Railroad.

Work on the Underground Railroad grew more dangerous in 1850 when Congress passed a new Fugitive Slave Act. The Slave Act said that runaway slaves found in the North had to be returned to their owners. It also created new punishments for those who assisted fugitives.

But Harriet Tubman continued her work despite the increased danger. Beginning in 1851, she made several trips back to Maryland and Virginia to guide other fugitive slaves, including members of her family, north. In 1856, Tubman made three excursions south. The last, in October of that year, found Tubman finishing one rescue mission and about to return to dangerous territory to begin another rescue mission as a guide on the Underground Railroad.

Read and Ponder

THE
FUGITIVE SLAVE LAW!

Which disregards all the ordinary securities of PERSONAL LIBERTY, which tramples on the Constitution, by its denial of the sacred rights of Trial by Jury, *Habeas Corpus*, and Appeal, and which enacts, that the Cardinal Virtues of Christianity shall be considered, in the eye of the law, as **CRIMES**, punishable with the severest penalties,— *Fines and Imprisonment.*

Freemen of Massachusetts, REMEMBER, That Samuel A. Elliott of Boston, voted for this law, that Millard Filmore, our whig President *approved* it and the Whig Journals of Massachusetts sustain them in this iniquity.

PRINTED AND FOR SALE AT THE SPY OFFICE.

The Fugitive Slave Act of 1850 became a major point of controversy after its passage by Congress.

SLAVES AND MASTERS

1

Slave owners forced enslaved people to do many types of work, including harsh physical labor, such as picking cotton.

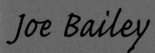

Joe Bailey

Talbot County, Maryland,
September 20, 1856

Joe Bailey watched the two slaves haul timber into the shipyard and nodded his approval. Joe was a slave too, one of the 40 working in the shipyard and on the farm owned by their master, William Hughlett. But Joe was no ordinary slave. He was the foreman of the shipyard, a manager of other slaves. When the harvest was brought in from the fields in a few weeks, he would supervise that too. Joe took great pride in his privileged position. The other slaves looked up to him almost as if he were their second master. However, Hughlett didn't own Joe. Joe's master had "rented" him out to Hughlett for the past six years.

As Joe mulled over these thoughts, his brother, Bill, who also worked for Hughlett, came up to him. "How's the boss man?" Bill asked.

"Aren't you supposed to be down at the mill?" Joe asked his brother.

"The work there's all done," replied Bill. "Thought I'd come up and see if you needed me here."

Joe looked up and saw their master approaching on horseback. "We don't need help," he said, "but you could ask Mr. Hughlett what he needs doing."

Hughlett, a tall man with a graying mustache, rode up and reined in his horse. He ignored Bill and spoke directly to Joe. "Things going smoothly up here, Joe?" he asked.

"As smooth as butter, Mr. Hughlett," replied his foreman.

"Good," said Hughlett. "I've got some news that I think you're going to like to hear, Joe. But I can't tell you yet. In a few days this business will be wrapped up and then I'll have a surprise for you. Until then, keep up the good work."

Joe smiled. Hughlett cast a sideways glance at Bill and then rode off toward his house.

"What was that all about?" Bill asked his brother.

Joe grinned and rubbed his bald head. "Sounds like I might be getting a promotion," he said.

Bill snorted. "The only promotion that would mean anything would be if he freed you. And *that* would be some surprise."

"Go on," replied Joe. "I think you're just a bit jealous, Bill."

"Why should I be jealous of a fool like you?" Bill shot back.

"And why am I a fool?" Joe asked.

"For trusting a white man," said his brother. Then he strode off. Joe watched him disappear along the banks of the nearby Choptank River.

He's the fool, he thought to himself. Then he turned his thoughts to the surprise his master had in store for him and wondered what it could be.

Harriet Tubman

Seaford, Delaware, October 12, 1856

Harriet Tubman was feeling nervous. She had made the journey along the Underground Railroad plenty of times in the past few years. She had brought many small groups of slaves north to freedom, but this time was different. Because of the difficulties facing her, she had made the bold decision to travel farther south to throw the slave catchers off her scent. But now she had to travel north again, facing the same dangers of capture, but this time for a greater distance.

The second dilemma she faced was Tilly, the young, light-skinned slave who clung to her arm as they walked. Tilly was running away from a master who planned to force her into marriage with a male slave she did not love. Harriet intended to see Tilly reunited with her true love, a man Harriet had led to freedom on a previous mission. Now she and Tilly were walking to the train depot in Seaford. They would board a train bound for the town of Camden, Delaware, and then travel to Pennsylvania, a free state, where Tilly would be safe.

Suddenly a gruff, deep voice caused Harriet to stop in her tracks.

"Hey, where are you women going?" asked a man's voice.

Harriet felt Tilly's grip on her arm tighten. She turned and saw a man standing nearby. Harriet recognized him as someone she had seen at the hotel they had stayed at the previous evening. She suspected he was a slave catcher, paid to capture runaways.

"You gonna answer me?" said the man.

"Going to the train to go back to master," said Harriet in a calm voice.

"He lets you ride on a train by yourself?" said the slave catcher. "That's one trusting master you have."

Harriet nodded. She could feel Tilly shaking as if she had a fever.

"I think you're lying to me," said the man, drawing closer. "You look to me like a couple of runaways."

Before the man could grab her arm, Harriet pulled a wrinkled paper from a pocket.

"What's that?" said the slave catcher.

"Pass from master," replied Harriet, as he snatched it from her hand. She watched his mouth curl into a frown as he read the pass. He thrust out his hand and Harriet took back the pass.

"Good day, mister," Harriet said as they headed for the depot.

"Is he gone, Moses?" whispered Tilly, using Harriet's nickname.

"Just keep walking," replied Harriet, keeping her voice calm. She'd had close calls before on rescue missions, but this was one of the closest.

Harriet Tubman, 1870

THE COST OF FREEDOM

2

Enslaved people were bought and sold in various ways, including at slave auctions. Families were often ripped apart when individuals were sold to different masters.

Eliza Manokey

Talbot County, Maryland,
October 20, 1856

Eliza Manokey unwrapped the piece of dried beef from the towel and began to gnaw on it hungrily. It was the first solid food she had eaten in two days. She got it from a freed black man who apologized that he couldn't let her stay at his home. He was afraid that the authorities would find out he was harboring a runaway slave and punish him. She understood. Those freed blacks who had given her shelter here and there over the past several months had been willing to take the risk, but she felt bad and afraid for them. As for sleeping outdoors, she was used to it. She had a sack and a blanket that one family she stayed with had given her.

Having no contacts on the Underground Railroad, Eliza had been unable to get very far from the plantation she had run away from. She felt like a trapped animal, living hand to mouth in the woods and hoping to find someone who could help her go north to Canada.

This part of Maryland's Eastern Shore was the territory of a woman known as Moses. Eliza hoped to find Moses leading other runaways north and join the group. But so far no one was able to tell her of Moses' movements or when she would be passing through the area. At age 42, Eliza was still in good health, but doubted she could survive the winter on her own. Already the days were growing shorter and the nights longer and colder. Whatever happened, she vowed to herself that she would not go back to her master.

She would rather die out here than be his slave again.

Finishing her dinner, she set the meat bone aside and did what she could to clean up, using the grass as a napkin. Then she pulled out her thin blanket and laid down to sleep.

Joe Bailey
Talbot County, Maryland,
October 23, 1856

The house slave welcomed Joe with a big smile and ushered him into the library. "Mr. Hughlett will be with you shortly, Joe," the older slave said. Joe sat down on a soft chair and looked around at the rows of books that lined the room. Then the door opened and Mr. Hughlett walked in briskly and sat down at the big oak desk by the large bay windows.

"Good to see you, Joe," he said. "I told you I had some good news for you and now that it's all settled, I can tell you what it is."

Joe leaned forward in his chair.

"Joe," continued Mr. Hughlett, "you've worked for me for six years now. You've been a hard worker and I've come to rely on you in many ways. I've never had a slave that showed the intelligence and good judgment that you have. You've become an important part of my operation and I felt it was time to make your place here a permanent one. So, I've offered to buy you from your master for a total of $2,000 and he's agreed. In a few days from now, Joe, you'll have a new master."

Joe was flabbergasted. Not only had Mr. Hughlett bought him from his master, but he had paid an unheard of price. Joe couldn't help but feel proud as he thanked Mr. Hughlett. Then Mr. Hughlett walked him out to the back door, explaining the details of his move to his new home. Joe walked out into the chilly fall air feeling as though he were on a cloud.

Two thousand dollars! he thought to himself. *Wait till old Bill hears that.*

Slave children behind plantation shacks, South Carolina, 1860

A SHOCK TO THE SYSTEM

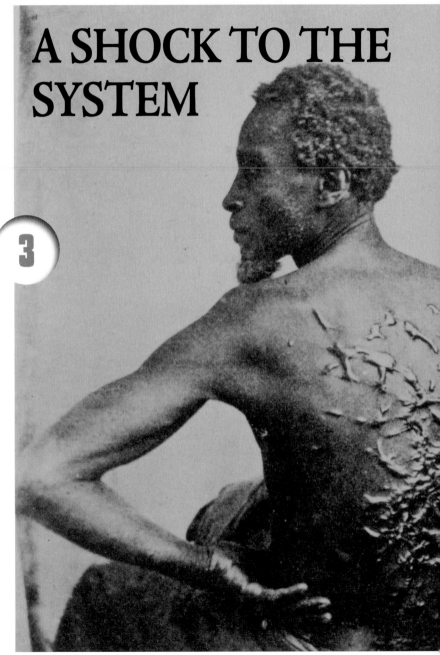

3

The whip-scarred back of Gordon, an escaped slave, Louisiana, 1863

Harriet Tubman

Eastern Shore, Maryland,
October 26, 1856

Harriet watched her sister, Rachel, approaching the large oak tree she stood under. It was just before dark descended, a good time of day for Rachel to come to their secret meeting without being seen by her master. It was safer for Harriet too. As long as she was in the United States, she could be recaptured and returned to a life of slavery at any time.

"How are you doing, Harriet?" asked Rachel, as they sat down on the dry grass.

"Busy as ever," replied her sister. Then she told Rachel about her adventure bringing Tilly north and how she had seen her off at Wilmington, Delaware. Her mission now was to convince Rachel to come north with her.

Harriet Tubman carried a pistol while working on
the Underground Railroad, but traded that weapon
in for a sharpshooter's rifle during the Civil War (1861–1865).

"Are you ready?" Harriet said, lowering her voice. There was no one to be seen in the shadows, but she was still cautious.

Rachel frowned and shook her head. "Not as long as my children can't go with me."

Harriet sighed. They had been through this before. Rachel would not leave the plantation without her two children, and taking them along on the long journey would be too difficult.

"I will come back for your children another time," said Harriet. "And that's a promise I will not break."

Rachel shook her head again, more firmly. "No," she repeated. "I'm not leaving here without them. And nothing you can say will change that."

Harriet could see that Rachel's mind was set. It pained her that she couldn't bring her sister north. She had already brought four of her brothers, their wives, and some of their children to freedom. Now the only family members who remained in Maryland were

Rachel and their parents, Ben and Rit. They wouldn't come with her either, but mostly because they felt they were too old to make the difficult trip.

The two sisters talked about family and their lives for a few more minutes and then embraced. "I'll be back again," Harriet said, letting Rachel know that she would not give up on her.

Rachel nodded. Then they went their separate ways in the growing darkness.

Joe Bailey

Talbot County, Maryland,
October 29, 1856

Joe waited patiently for his new master in the barn. He didn't know why Mr. Hughlett wanted to meet with him here, but it didn't matter. The important thing was that now he had Hughlett for his master, not just for the working day but 24 hours a day. His life could only get better in Hughlett's hands, he thought.

He heard the barn door creak and saw his new master enter. Two things about Hughlett surprised him. He had a dark scowl on his face and in his hand he held a whip. The man's expression brightened slightly when he saw Joe. *Has he just come from disciplining another one of his slaves?* Joe wondered.

"Something wrong, Mr. Hughlett?" Joe asked.

"No, Joe," said his master. "But I've got to do something I don't like to do."

Joe looked at the whip and he felt a chill trickle down his spine.

"What's that?" he asked.

"Joe, I want you to strip off your shirt."

Joe couldn't believe the words he was hearing. "Why?" he asked.

Hughlett was busy rolling up his shirt sleeves. "Just do as I tell you, Joe," he said, his voice growing colder.

This is a just a bad dream. This can't be happening, thought Joe. He couldn't believe this was the same man who had taken such good care of him for six years, the master for whom he had worked so hard all that time.

"Have I done something wrong?" Joe asked. "Have I done something you didn't like?"

Hughlett looked up from the whip. "No, Joe," he said. "You've done nothing wrong. But that doesn't matter. You see, when I buy a slave I've got to give him a lesson. That lesson is to make sure he knows his place and never gets a thought in his head about disobeying me. And I can't make any exceptions. Not even for you, Joe."

"But I never would do anything that would make you do this thing, Mr. Hughlett," he protested, his voice growing louder. "You must know that."

"That may be so, Joe," said Hughlett, flexing the whip in his hand. "But like I told you, I can't make any exceptions."

Joe unbuttoned his shirt and let it fall to the floor.

In their fight against slavery, abolitionists created many illustrations
depicting the horrors enslaved people suffered in the United States.

"Now lie down on your stomach, Joe," said Hughlett.

Joe did as he was told. The rich odor of straw and freshly cut wood filled his nostrils. He braced himself. The whip lashed his back with a sharp sting. He didn't cry out or speak for the nine more lashes that ripped away at his skin. Then it was over.

"You can get up, Joe, and clean yourself off," said Hughlett. "And I pray that we'll never have to meet again like this."

Then Hughlett was gone.

Joe soaked a rag in the nearby water trough and began washing the blood away from his torn, tender skin. It wasn't just the physical pain that made him ache, but the humiliation, the shame. Bill had been right.

He knew now that he had been fooling himself. It didn't matter how much power he had over Hughlett's other slaves. Before his master he was as powerless as any of them.

As he dried himself off with a second rag, he thought about his master's last words. *No*, he thought to himself. *We'll never meet again this way. Because I won't be here.*

I'm going to get as far away from this place as I can, no matter what the cost.

ESCAPE PLANS

In 1850 there were an estimated 3.2 million enslaved people living in the United States.

William Hughlett lay in bed unable to sleep. No matter how hard he tried, he could not get Joe Bailey off his mind. Most of his slaves came to his place as strangers, having just been newly bought. Giving them their whipping left him with no feeling whatsoever. But after six years of good work from Joe, this case felt more complicated.

Hughlett decided that giving Joe his whipping had hurt him as much as it had Joe. Then he thought about how few times he'd needed to give a second whipping to those slaves who tasted the lash. They knew who was master and gave him little trouble after that. Aside from that, none of his slaves had ever run away, unlike those of many other slave owners on the Eastern Shore.

Many local runaway slaves had been encouraged and helped by the woman they called Moses. To Hughlett she was no Moses, but a devil sent by Satan himself to steal the property of honest, hardworking men like him. He wished he could lay a whip on the back of this Moses woman. He would watch the blood run freely down her legs with not a drop of sympathy. As for Joe, he would continue to keep him in the high position he was in. He'd ask his wife to give Joe one of his old coats for the winter. It would help make up for the whipping. Feeling satisfied that this settled the matter, Hughlett rolled over and went to sleep.

Joe pulled his little boat up onto the shore and made the short walk to Ben Ross' cabin. It had taken him only a brief time to row down the river to the plantation where Ben Ross worked. Ben had been given his freedom years earlier by his masters, although his wife and children were still slaves. Joe had known Ben for a long time, but he hadn't come to catch up. He was looking for Ben's daughter, known as Moses, who had run away some years earlier. He hoped Ben could tell him where she was. It was she who could help him make the long journey north to freedom. He knocked on the door of Ben's cabin and a tired voice said, "Come in." Ben was sitting in a chair at a small wooden table. A candle's glow dimly lit the cabin.

The older man was pleased to see Joe and asked how he was. Joe told him about the whipping and Ben clucked his tongue in sympathy. "I'm sorry to hear about your misery," he said. "But why did you come to me?"

Joe looked Ben straight in the eye. "Next time Moses comes, let me know," he said. "I have to talk to her."

Ben nodded his gray head. "I'll deliver the message," he said.

Joe knew that Ben understood. When someone came asking for Moses, it was for only one reason — that person was ready to travel on the Underground Railroad.

When planning an escape, enslaved people had to make difficult choices about whom to bring along. It wasn't always possible for children or elderly people to make the dangerous journey on the Underground Railroad.

THE JOURNEY BEGINS

5

Runaway slaves did whatever they could to hide and stay safe until they could reach safe houses on the Underground Railroad.

Joe Bailey

Talbot County, Maryland, November 3, 1856

Joe was directing workers when his brother Bill came striding in. He hadn't talked to Bill since the whipping and had gone out of his way to avoid him. He didn't want Bill to know what had happened and

get him mixed up in his plan to run away. Bill, like him, had a wife and children. He knew how some slave masters took out their anger over a runaway on the family members he left behind. That's why he figured the less Bill knew about what he was going to do, the better.

"What's wrong, brother?" Bill asked in a low voice, as he approached Joe. "Why have you been avoiding me?"

"I've just been busy," said Joe, with a straight face. "That's all."

Bill looked around at the other slaves and lowered his voice another notch. "I've heard rumors that something happened between you and Master," he said.

Joe gave an uneasy laugh. "You should know better than to listen to slave gossip, Bill," he replied.

Before Joe knew what was happening, Bill slipped around behind him and pulled up the tail end of his shirt. Joe cried out as Bill took a good look at his back.

"Just as I thought," he said. "So old Hughlett gave you a dose of the same medicine we've been getting."

There was no bitterness in his brother's voice, and Joe immediately regretted not being more honest with him.

"There's another rumor flying around the farm," Bill continued. "It says you're thinking about taking a trip north with Moses."

Joe could see there was no longer any point in lying. "I just wanted to protect you," he said.

"I don't need protection, Joe," said Bill. "The fact is, I want to go with you."

"You've got a family," Joe reminded him.

"So do you," said Bill.

"I'm planning to come back for them later," Joe said.

"Then we'll come back together," said Bill stubbornly.

Joe sighed. It was clear his brother was as determined to get away from the slave life as he was. He put one hand on Bill's shoulder. "All right," he said. "We go together."

Harriet Tubman

Caroline County, Maryland,
November 12, 1856

Harriet looked across the table at the three men who sat staring at her, ready to listen to every word she had to say. Peter Pennington was a slave her father had brought to her a few days earlier. The other two, brothers from a neighboring farm, she was meeting for the first time. But they both knew her father and he spoke well of them.

"It won't be easy," she told them. "Once they find you're missing, they are going to be hunting for you. It's 90 miles to Wilmington, Delaware, and they'll be after us every step of the way. There'll be friends helping us, providing food and shelter, but there will be difficult times too. There may be times when you wonder if this is worth it and if you'll get caught and sent back to your masters. So if you have doubts or don't think you're up to it, now's the time to say so."

The Bailey brothers and Peter Pennington exchanged looks. "We're ready to follow you all the way, Moses," said Joe, speaking for the three of them.

"How are we going to protect ourselves if a slave catcher tries to take us?" asked Peter.

Harriet pulled a long revolver from under her cape and laid it down on the table. "This is our protection," she said.

Bill stared at the gun. "You ever shoot a man, Moses?" he asked.

"Haven't had to yet," she replied. "But if it comes to that I would. And there's something else you should know."

They leaned forward to hear her better.

"Once we start out there'll be no going back," she continued. "Anyone tries to leave, to turn back, they'll find themselves looking down the barrel of this revolver."

The cabin was silent as the men stared at each other. "Now go back to your homes," Harriet told them.

"And don't tell a soul what you're planning to do. Not your wife. Not your children. No one."

Joe nodded. "When are we leaving?"

"Saturday night," she said. "That's the best time. No one will miss you on Sunday, your day off. That'll give us a head start on them. I'll send you word where to meet me."

ON THE RUN

6

Enslaved families were typically housed in one- or two-room buildings with dirt floors. Slave owners often didn't take care of these cabins, unconcerned if the roofs leaked or the chimneys caught fire.

William Hughlett

Talbot County, Maryland,
November 17, 1856

Hughlett squeezed his whip in his fist as he paced back and forth in the barn. He had been betrayed — not once, but twice. He had treated Joe so well for six years, and now this trusted slave wasn't in his cabin, wasn't anywhere to be found. Hughlett was sure Joe had run away, and his brother Bill had gone with him. It also appeared that Turpin Wright's slave, Peter Pennington, had run away with Joe and Bill. Joe and Bill's wives claimed to be as shocked by their sudden disappearance as Hughlett was. But he was sure the women were lying. He had been a fool to put his faith in any slave. But the runaways wouldn't get far.

He slapped the whip against his leg. "Elias!" he cried, and the house slave came running into the barn. "Saddle up my horse," he commanded. He was getting over the emotion of the moment and starting to think clearly. He would ride to the home of John Henry, Bill Bailey's owner, and the home of Turpin Wright to tell them the bad news. Then they would form a search party. They'd find them. He wasn't about to lose a slave that he'd agreed to pay $2,000 for.

Eliza Manokey

Talbot County, Maryland,
November 17, 1856

Eliza Manokey pressed her ear against the cold ground and listened, determined to find Moses. She had received word from a local slave that Moses was in the area and heading north with a small party of runaways. This was her chance, maybe her last chance, to escape.

She knew the Underground Railroad only ran at night. Traveling on foot during the day was too dangerous. For the last several nights she had been waiting along the route she was told Moses would be coming on, looking and listening. So far she had seen and heard nothing.

But now, as she lay on the wet grass, Eliza heard sounds — footsteps moving quickly. The sounds grew louder and louder. Eliza stood up and saw at a distance a group of figures in the moonlight. She counted the shadows, *one, two, three, four*. As the figures drew closer she could see them more clearly — a woman, short and stout, flanked by three taller men. Hoping this was Moses and her party, Eliza ran toward the group across the darkened field.

Harriet Tubman

Harriet stopped dead in her tracks as she saw the woman racing toward her. The woman appeared to be middle-aged, and in a weakened condition that only made her look older. Before she reached the group and fell to her knees, Harriet knew she was a runaway and why she was there.

"Moses, Moses," the woman cried, tears flooding her eyes. "Please, take me with you."

Peter Pennington stared at the woman. "Who is she?" he asked.

"How long have you been out here, sister?" Harriet asked in a soft voice.

"Since summer," the woman said, her voice and body shaking.

Harriet pulled the woman to her feet and looked her over.

"We can't take her with us," said Bill Bailey. "Look at her. She'll only slow us down."

Harriet turned on Bill. "You let me be the judge of that," she said. "I'm the conductor here. You're just a passenger along for the ride."

She leaned toward the woman. "What's your name?"

"Eliza Manokey," the woman replied.

"Are you strong enough, Eliza Manokey, to go all night — every night — until we reach Wilmington?" Harriet asked her.

Eliza nodded her head vigorously. "I promise I won't slow you down, Moses. If I do, you can shoot me."

Harriet laughed. "Don't think there'll be any need for that," she said. "Come on. Let's get moving."

The men said nothing but fell in step behind the two women. The travelers spoke little as they continued on their journey.

Harriet knew that was good — they were saving their strength for the long road ahead. Harriet thought about how just seven years ago, she, like this Eliza, had followed the same path, alone, and just as afraid.

A family of enslaved people on Smith's Plantation, Beaufort, South Carolina, 1862

THE PRICE OF FREEDOM

7

It was very difficult to permanently escape from slavery. Runaways were tracked by dogs as they faced other difficulties, such as finding adequate food and shelter.

Hughlett reined in his horse and waited impatiently for the other riders. John Henry and Turpin Wright had brought along several men who worked for them. They all carried guns.

"Which way?" asked Henry, gazing out over the flat potato fields that surrounded them.

"Let's stay on the road," said Hughlett. "They may hide in the woods, but eventually they'll have to come out into this open country. Then we'll catch them."

Wright looked doubtful. "But they could hide out for days," he said.

"They can't hide forever," replied Hughlett. "If they want to get to the north, the only way is through Wilmington. And to get there they have to cross the Christina River Bridge. It's the only route across the river. If we don't find them along the way we can beat them to the bridge and wait for them there."

Wright shook his head. "There's no telling how long that could take," he said. "I can't be away from my farm that long."

Both Hughlett and Henry looked at him with disgust.

"You want your slave back, don't you?" said Henry.

Hughlett waved a hand to quiet Henry. "You can turn back if you want, Turpin. There's plenty of slave catchers up there who'd be happy to catch your Peter for you, for a price."

"All right," said Wright, after some thought. "But I'll stay with you for a day or two. Maybe we'll catch them on the road."

Hughlett doubted that. The Moses woman, from everything he'd heard, was clever, too smart to be caught easily. But he was determined to get his Joe back, no matter how long it took.

"Let's not waste any more time sitting here talking," said Hughlett and slapped the side of his horse. The others quickly fell in behind him.

Harriet Tubman

Talbot County, Maryland,
November 18, 1856

Harriet brushed the dirt from her face and sat up in the potato field. She had hidden in potato holes before, but never this close to her pursuers. The horsemen hunting for them had been only a few feet from where she lay. She brushed the damp soil from her clothes and rose slowly to her feet, telling the others to get up. Four more bodies rose up from the potato field as if they were revived corpses in a cemetery.

"I hope this is the last time I have to lie buried in a potato hole," said Peter, spitting dirt from his mouth.

Reverend Samuel Green, 1860

"Don't count on it," replied Harriet. "When the slave catchers are out, you hide wherever you can." It had been a mistake to be out in daylight, but she was pushing to get as far away from the Hughlett place as possible. Now she saw that had been a mistake.

"Not safe to travel on the road anymore," she said. "Not until it's dark. Best that we split up and then meet at Reverend Green's house by nightfall. He's expecting us."

She gave Joe the map she'd made. Harriet couldn't read or write, but she'd copied it from a map Green had once made for her. "Follow this," she said to the three men. "Eliza and I will meet up with you after dark at the Green place."

Then they went their separate ways into the woods beyond the field. Eliza held Harriet's hand for a time and then fell in line behind her. "Will we be safe at Reverend Green's?" she asked.

Harriet smiled for the first time that day. "As safe as at any station on the Underground Railroad," she said.

Samuel Green

The Reverend Green looked out his window at the old woman approaching his house. She wore a large sunbonnet that covered her face and hobbled along at a slow pace. Behind her walked another woman, younger, walking more briskly, although she kept pace behind the older one.

Green sighed. These were not members of his congregation in East New Market come to call. There could be only one reason why they were coming to his house. They had to be runaway slaves looking for a safe house. Green was used to such visitors. He had been a stationmaster for several years now and had sheltered dozens of fugitives on their journey to freedom in Canada. He knew the journey well and the difficulties to be faced. He himself had been a slave, but hadn't had to run away to gain his liberty. He had bought his freedom at the age of 30 with money he'd saved. His two children remained slaves, but he bought his wife's freedom a decade later. Unfortunately, their two children were sold off to another slaveholder five years after that. One of them, Sam Green, Jr., ran away to Canada with the help of Harriet Tubman. For this Green would be eternally grateful to Tubman.

The two women were almost at the door now and Green was startled. The old woman suddenly developed a spring in her step. As he opened the front door, she removed her sunbonnet.

"Well, Harriet," said Green, recognizing his old friend, "this is a surprise. I should have known it was you."

"Can't take any chances," said Harriet Tubman, smiling. "You never know who might be watching. Reverend, I'd like you to meet a dear friend of mine. We'd sure appreciate you putting us up for the night."

"You know you're always welcome," said Green. "Any more in your party?"

"Three men," said Harriet. "They should be along shortly."

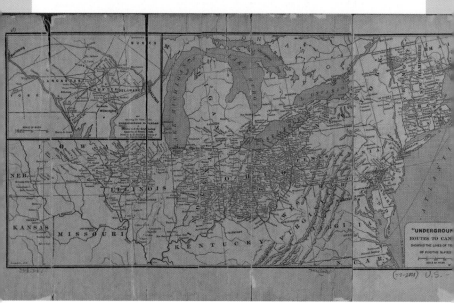

Underground Railroad stationmasters helped runaways with items such as maps showing safe routes to Canada. If discovered by the authorities, these items could be dangerous for their owners.

William Hughlett

Near Wilmington, Delaware,
November 19, 1856

Hughlett watched with satisfaction as the sheriff's deputy nailed the wanted posters to a tree, one of the many leading into town. The road was a main one for travelers and everyone heading for Wilmington would see the posters. They were being nailed up not only on trees, but also barns and store walls. The rewards would be enough motivation to put everyone on the lookout for the runaways and their leader.

The wanted posters for Bill Bailey and Peter Pennington offered $300 and $800 respectively for their capture. But Hughlett had posted a far higher reward for Bill's brother, Joe. The poster read, "Reward of $1,500 and all expenses for his return to the Easton jail." Once captured, Hughlett intended to take Joe from the jail and bring him home, where he would receive the whipping of his life. Just thinking about the slave's betrayal made Hughlett's blood boil. He turned his head to see another poster the deputy was attaching to the tree. The person on this poster was perhaps the most wanted man or woman in Maryland. Hughlett read it approvingly.

WANTED

Harriet Tubman

REWARD $12,000

Laws in some states, including Delaware and Maryland, allowed
pursuers to kill runaway slaves who refused to surrender.

THE BRIDGE

100 DOLLS. REWARD

RAN AWAI

From me, on Saturday, the 19th inst.,

Negro Boy Robert Porte

aged **19**; heavy, stoutly mad dark chesnut complexio rather sullen countenanc with a down look; face large; head low on shoulders. I believe he entered the City Washington on Sunday evening, 20th inst. has changed his dress probably, except boots, which were new and heavy.

I will give **$50** if taken and secured in District of Columbia, or **$100** if taken no of the District, and secured in each case delivered before the reward shall be good.

Dr. J. W. THOMAS.

Pomunky P. O., Charles Co., Md.

Night was falling when Joe Bailey and the other fugitives left the last safe house and headed toward the bridge that would take them out of slave country and farther on the road to freedom. The Christina River separated Maryland, a slave state, from Delaware. Harriet had told Joe that Delaware still had slave catchers on the prowl and that they wouldn't be truly safe until they reached Philadelphia, Pennsylvania.

Joe feared being recaptured as much as any of them. He knew William Hughlett would be furious with him for running away when he had just bought him at such a dear price. Worse than a whipping, his new master might sell him off to a southern slave owner who would demote him to a field hand, picking cotton all day in the hot sun.

Joe tried to think about his future with hope, but all that dissolved when they passed a tree covered with wanted posters.

"Looks like you're worth a lot more on the slave market than I am," said Bill, looking at the posters.

Harriet stepped between them and ripped down the poster of Joe with a swipe of her hand.

"You can't tear them all down," Joe said to her. "I'm finished. Hughlett won't rest until he's got me back."

"He's not getting you back," insisted Harriet. "So stop thinking that."

Joe just shook his head. "You best leave me behind and move on," he said.

Harriet stared at Joe and planted her arms on his broad shoulders.

"Nobody's being left behind," she said.

"You forget about the past and start thinking of a new future for yourself, Joe."

"I'll try," said Joe. But in his heart he had all but given up any hope of freedom.

Hughlett stood surrounded by people.
He saw there were all sorts of slave catchers,
vigilantes, and just plain curiosity seekers
looking to see what all the excitement was
about. Word had quickly spread that Harriet
Tubman was trying to reach Wilmington
with a small band of fugitive slaves and that
he, Hughlett, had arranged for guards on the
bridge to catch them if they appeared.

The posters and publicity had done their
work well. There was no way Tubman and her
runaways could get across the bridge without
being detected. And there was no other way
they could cross into Delaware from where
they were. The trap was set and now it was just
a matter of time.

A BLOCK IN THE ROAD

Harriet Tubman's brave leadership in the face of danger along the Underground Railroad brought her great praise among abolitionists.

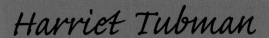

Harriet Tubman

"What are we going to do, Moses?"
asked Bill Bailey.

For once, Harriet didn't have a ready
answer. They had made it this far without
a hitch, and now, after spying the heavily
guarded bridge, they could go no farther.
There was only one person Harriet could
think of whom she could turn to for help.
It was Thomas Garrett. He was one of
the most famous stationmasters on the
Underground Railroad and a good friend.
Garrett lived in Wilmington, Delaware,
and she had to get word to him at once.

The other fugitives stood waiting for
an answer to Bill's question.

"Have you got a plan, Moses?"
asked Eliza.

"Yes," lied Harriet, "but it will take a day to work it out. In the meantime, we'll stay at different safe houses. In the morning, we'll make our move."

Then she led them away, planning to ask one of the stationmasters they'd be staying with to send a man to Wilmington to ask Garrett for help. She hoped he'd respond quickly. Every hour they remained in Maryland, the danger of capture grew.

Thomas Garrett

Wilmington, Delaware,
November 23, 1856

Thomas Garrett was in a quandary. An hour earlier he had received word from a black messenger that Harriet Tubman was waiting to cross over into Wilmington, but that the bridge was heavily guarded. Garrett was a Quaker, a member of a religious sect that was opposed to war and slavery. Since moving to

Wilmington with his family nearly 35 years before, Garrett had helped bring hundreds of fugitives to freedom. Like Harriet, he was totally committed to the abolitionist cause and was fearless in his work. Garrett was a white man, but that hadn't stopped other white southerners from beating him, throwing him from a moving train, and threatening to kill him for helping fugitive slaves. Eight years earlier he had been arrested, tried and convicted of aiding runaway slaves, and fined $5,000, leaving him with few resources. But he refused to stop working for a cause he believed in.

Now, he had to help one of his dearest colleagues and the fugitives she was guiding. But how? He hadn't a clue of what he could do to get them across the bridge and into Delaware. But Harriet was counting on him, and he couldn't let her down. If she should be caught by the slave catchers he knew she faced a far worse fate than a fine.

As he pondered the problem, two wagons rolled by. They were driven by two free black men he knew who worked for a bricklaying business. They had finished their work for the day in Maryland and were returning to Wilmington with empty wagons. Looking at the wagons, Garrett suddenly had an idea.

He waved for the driver of the first wagon, whose name was Otis, to stop.

"I need thy help, Otis," he said to him.

"What kind of help, Mr. Garrett?" asked the wagon driver.

"Would thee be willing to carry some extra cargo when you go over the bridge tomorrow morning?" Garrett asked.

Otis knew Garrett's business and that "cargo" was a code word for escaped slaves.

"I'm always willing to help you in your work, Mr. Garrett," said the bricklayer.

Thomas Garrett

A NEW PLAN

Underground Railroad agents built secret hiding places for runaways in buildings and vehicles such as wagons.

Harriet Tubman

Near the Christina River Bridge, Maryland, November 25, 1856, 5:00 p.m.

Harriet watched the two wagons pull up in the growing twilight. At first, she wondered where

she and her cargo would be able to
hide in the wagon beds, which were
full of bricks.

"We'll be crushed to death under all
those bricks!" Eliza said, clearly terrified.

Otis introduced himself to the group
with a sweep of his hat and jumped
down from the wagon seat. "No need
to worry about that," he said. "We've
got a nice place for each of you folks
on board." He and his companion
pulled some of the bricks off the wagon,
revealing a hidden wooden compartment
underneath. The space, to Harriet,
looked no bigger than a coffin.

"Climb on in, Miss," Otis said to
Eliza. "We've got to get a move on."

"I'll go first," Harriet told Otis.
Before she took his hand to help her up,
she patted Eliza's cheek. "It won't be for
long," she told her gently. "Just until we
get to Wilmington. You'll be all right.
There's no other way."

Eliza nodded and the other men looked on as Harriet stuffed her body into the small compartment. Otis left the rectangular door open so she could see that the others were loaded in their compartments. Then she saw Otis poke his head into the tiny opening.

"You all right in there, Moses?" he asked.

"I'm packed in tight," said Harriet. "But I'm sure I'll live."

Otis laughed.

"You just be careful not to hit too many bumps," she said, as Otis closed the door and she was cast into utter darkness.

Joe Bailey

Near the Christina River Bridge, Maryland, November 25, 1856, 6:00 p.m.

Joe lay in the stuffy darkness, his mind filled with terrible thoughts. He imagined being dragged out of his hiding place by men at the bridge and sent back to Mr. Hughlett's in chains. He feared for himself, but for his companions and his rescuer as well. He was the one whom Hughlett was after and because of him, they might all be captured. Why did he run away in the first place?

Suddenly he heard singing and laughing. He recognized the voices of Otis and the other wagon driver. He couldn't believe his ears. They must be nearing the bridge to Wilmington and they were deliberately raising a ruckus that would surely draw the attention of the guards!

Had they lost their minds?

Joe could feel cold sweat running down his body.

Suddenly, without warning, the wagon came to a grinding halt.

DANGEROUS CROSSING

Runaways who were able to arm themselves could sometimes use their weapons to keep pursuers away and continue their escape.

A Sherriff's Deputy

Christina River Bridge, Wilmington, Delaware, November 25, 1856, 6:05 p.m.

The deputy lowered his rifle as the black man in the seat of the lead wagon stopped his singing and lowered his hat as a greeting.

"You're sure in a merry mood tonight, Otis, aren't you?" he said.

Otis grinned. "We're always in a good mood when we're coming back from a long day's work, Sheriff."

The deputy didn't respond to the promotion in rank. He knew that Otis knew full well he was a deputy. He gazed over the wagon and its heavy load.

"Bringing a lot of bricks back with you tonight," the deputy said. "Why's that?"

Otis scratched his head and put his hat back on. "Well, we didn't get as much work done today as we wanted to, Sheriff," he explained. "But we'll make up for it tomorrow."

The deputy smiled. *Typical, shiftless Negroes,* he thought. *Even these freed ones are just as lazy as the slaves.*

"Can we get going now?" asked Otis politely. "Got to get home for dinner."

"Sure, Otis," said the deputy. "Go on home."

Otis cried, "Git!" to the horses and gave the reins a yank. The wagon started over the bridge, its wheels creaking. Then Otis began

Runaways on the Underground Railroad typically preferred to travel at night.

to sing, louder than before, the other driver joining in.

The deputy shook his head and turned to another deputy standing nearby. "That's all they're good for," he said with a sneer. "Singing and laughing. Not a thought in their heads."

His companion nodded in agreement. "How long do you figure we have to stand guard here?" he asked a moment later.

"Not much longer," replied the deputy. "Our replacements will be coming on soon. But I doubt those runaways will try anything tonight. They know we'd catch them as soon as they appeared."

Harriet Tubman

Wilmington, Delaware,
November 25, 1856, 7:00 p.m.

Harriet couldn't feel her legs. They were so cramped in the tiny compartment that the blood flow felt like it had stopped. She was wondering when Otis and the other driver were going to stop and let them out when all of a sudden the wagon came to an abrupt halt. A moment later the compartment door opened and Otis' smiling face appeared.

"Why'd you wait so long?" said Harriet, as he helped her out of the wagon.

"Didn't feel safe stopping until we were outside of town," explained Otis. "Wilmington's crawling with slave catchers tonight. You sure raised a ruckus with your cargo this time, Moses."

"Well, don't stand there gabbing," she said. "Get the others out."

Otis and his companion did so and soon they were all standing around, rubbing their aching arms and legs.

"Mr. Garrett arranged for another wagon to take you on to Philadelphia," Otis told Harriet. "It's waiting down the road just a piece. Didn't want to draw too much attention by having them alongside us."

"You thank Mr. Garrett for me," Harriet said. "And tell him next time I'm in Wilmington I'll be stopping by for a visit."

"I'm sure he'll be happy to hear that, Moses," said Otis.

A family of fugitives traveling by wagon, 1863

Harriet thanked him and they headed down the road a short distance, where the other wagon awaited them.

"Can't we stay here and rest?" asked Eliza.

"Sorry, sister," said Harriet, taking her arm. "It isn't safe to stay here in Wilmington another minute. And don't you worry. This time we can ride on top of the wagon."

Bill Bailey rubbed his arm. "Just as long as there aren't any bricks to sit on," he said.

"Looks like we're in luck," said Peter Pennington. "That wagon is filled with nice, soft straw."

Even Joe Bailey laughed when he heard that. Harriet was pleased to see Joe was in a better mood. But they were still a long way from Canada and freedom.

Transportation, such as horses and wagons, could be a great help to runaway slaves.

THE FINAL PUSH

The hope of reaching true freedom in Canada helped many fugitives continue a difficult journey.

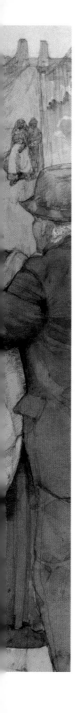

Joe Bailey

Over a long but uneventful two days, the fugitives moved through Philadelphia and then made their way to New York City. Joe Bailey was finally beginning to relax and feel that the worst of his journey was behind him. In just a few days, Moses kept telling him, they would be in Canada and he'd be a free man.

Now they were about to meet Underground Railroad agent Oliver Johnson. He would tell them the details of the last leg of their journey. Harriet led them into Johnson's office. Joe saw a large, good-natured man sitting behind a desk. He rose as they entered and embraced Harriet. Then he shook hands with each of them.

"Joe, it's a great pleasure to shake the hand of a man who is worth $1,500 to his master," he said.

Joe groaned softly and his hand went limp. Johnson's joke referred to the reward for him on the wanted posters. They had seen these posters all over Maryland, but they must have also spread to New York. How else would Johnson know about the price on his head?

Joe's old fears returned like a swarm of bees buzzing around his brain. He felt a chill run through his body. Harriet and Johnson were talking animatedly, but their words meant nothing to Joe. He was once again surrounded by shadows of fear.

Harriet was worried. While the others were growing excited in their anticipation of reaching Canada, Joe remained alone and apart, lost in a world of doom and dread. They were now in Syracuse, a city in upstate New York, and about to receive the details of their train ride into Canada from William E. Abbott, treasurer of the local Fugitive Aid Society.

"When can we leave for Niagara?" Harriet asked Abbott. They would travel farther upstate on a train that would cross over the suspension bridge spanning Niagara Falls. Then they would travel to the Canadian town of St. Catharines, their final destination.

"Harriet, I'm afraid we will not be able to take you directly to Niagara by train," he explained. "You see, our funds are very low right now. We will have to send your party overland by coach and wagon to halfway houses on the route north. You'll get to the Niagara bridge, but it will just take a little longer."

This was not good news. Harriet knew the others would not be discouraged by this slight delay, but for Joe it would be devastating. He was sitting on a chair in a corner of the room and it was clear he had heard every word of their conversation. He held his head in his hands, unmoving.

"It'll be all right, Joe," she said gently, patting his head. "I give you my word."

But Joe said nothing. He just sat there, a portrait of despair.

New York City, 1856

FREE AT LAST

The Niagara River was often the last crossing for people escaping slavery in the United States. From the early 1800s until the end of the Civil War in 1865, thousands of fugitives passed over the bridge as they traveled to freedom in Canada.

Eliza Manokey

Near Niagara Falls,
December 3, 1856, 2:30 p.m.

It had taken a few days to reach the border region, but now they were finally here. Eliza gazed out the train window in wonderment. She had never seen anything as beautiful in her life as Niagara Falls. The water poured down as if from a great open faucet, falling into the river below. The mist that arose from the falls with the sunlight upon it created a rainbow. Eliza saw it as a good omen. She only wished that Joe would share in their happiness. He sat alone, a few car seats away, his head still in his hands, refusing to look.

Harriet began to sing a spiritual she had taught them earlier. Eliza and Bill and Peter joined in:

I'm on my way to Canada,
That cold and dreary land;
The sad effects of slavery
I can't no longer stand.
I've served my master all my days,
Without a dime's reward;
And now I'm forced to run away,
To flee the lash abroad.
Farewell, old master, don't think hard of me,
I'll travel on to Canada,
Where all the slaves are free.

Eliza looked to see if Joe was joining in the singing. But his head remained in his hands. Harriet rose from her seat and went to where he sat. Eliza started up the song again and the two men joined in heartily.

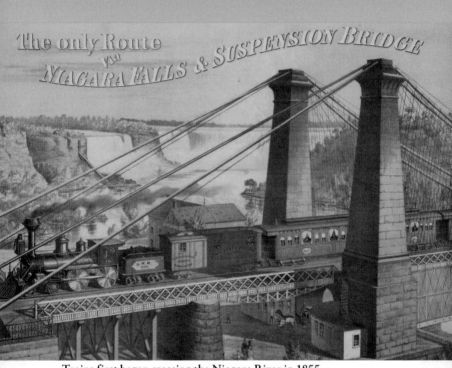

Trains first began crossing the Niagara River in 1855, allowing more people to cross over from the United States to Canada.

Joe Bailey

Near Niagara Falls,
December 3, 1856, 2:40 p.m.

Joe heard the singing, but it brought no joy to his heart. He felt that Hughlett would not rest until he had gotten him back, even if it meant chasing him all the way to Canada. Suddenly he felt a hand on his shoulder. He looked up to see Moses standing over him.

"Joe, listen to me, and listen good," she said, her face in his face. "You have shaken the lion's paw!"

He stared at her, not comprehending her words. "Hughlett can't touch you anymore," she said.

"No slave catcher can get you now. We've crossed the international border into Canada. You're a free man, Joe. Don't you see, you're free!"

96

Joe's body shuddered. He looked out the window. He could see the rainbow that arched over the bridge. Its far end was in Canada. Harriet's words started to sink into his brain. Could she be right? She had always told him the truth before. He had to believe her.

A conductor passed them, heading for the front of the train as it approached the St. Catharines station. Joe, without a word, jumped from his seat and followed him into the next car and then off the train. He turned and saw Harriet racing after him, but he lost her in the crowd of well-wishers, both black and white, who filled the small train station. He rushed past them and fell to his knees on the ground, his hands clawing at the rich, dark soil of Canada. He looked up and saw Harriet standing over him, tears welling in his eyes.

"Only one more journey for me, Moses, and that's to heaven!" he cried.

Harriet pulled a handkerchief from her pocket and wiped away Joe's tears. "That's all fine, you old fool, but you might have at least looked at the falls first and then gone to heaven afterward!"

Freed former slaves, Richmond, Virginia, 1865

EPILOGUE

Harriet Tubman continued to ride along the "liberty lines" of the Underground Railroad. By her last trip in 1860, she had journeyed south a total of 19 times and helped more than 300 enslaved people gain their freedom. The tensions between the slave states of the South and the free states of the North finally erupted into war in early 1861. The Union of the North fought the Southern Confederacy of states in a bloody campaign that lasted four long years. During the war, Tubman served the Union as a hospital nurse, a scout for raiding parties, and a spy in Confederate territory.

On January 1, 1863, President Abraham Lincoln issued the Emancipation Proclamation, declaring free all enslaved people in Confederate held areas. But because Confederate states did not accept Lincoln's authority, true freedom didn't come until the war ended. When the Union won the war and the 13th Amendment to the Constitution was passed, slavery was finally ended in the United States.

Abolitionists from different backgrounds helped
strengthen the Underground Railroad.

Tubman continued to work tirelessly for freed
African Americans. From her home in Auburn, New
York, she raised money for schools for black children.
In 1908, she founded the John Brown Home for
Aged and Indigent Negroes. She died on March 10,
1913, at the age of about 92.

Joe and Bill Bailey built new lives for
themselves in St. Catharines. Peter Pennington
did so too, later moving to the settlement

Once the Union won the Civil War in 1865, the Emancipation
Proclamation finally began to take effect in southern slave states.

of Sarnia, where he worked as a fish dealer. All three men were recruited by Tubman to join the movement against slavery led by abolitionist John Brown, who was a friend of Tubman's. Fortunately, they decided not to participate in Brown's attack on the arsenal at Harpers Ferry, Virginia, in 1859. A number of Brown's followers were killed in the failed rebellion and Brown himself was later executed. Nothing is known of the later lives of the Baileys and Pennington. Neither is anything known of the life of Eliza Manokey after she arrived in Canada.

Ben Ross, Tubman's father, and her mother, Rit, finally made the trip to freedom with their daughter in 1857. Harriet moved her parents into a house in Auburn in 1859, and Ross died in 1871. Unfortunately, her sister, Rachel, never left Talbot County, and died, still enslaved, in 1859. The fate of her two children is unknown.

William Hughlett's business did not suffer after the loss of Joe Bailey. He continued to thrive as one of the wealthiest men and largest slaveholders on Maryland's Eastern Shore. He died in 1885.

The Reverend Samuel Green continued to serve as a stationmaster on the Underground Railroad until he was arrested in 1857 and sentenced to ten years in prison for possessing a copy of Harriet Beecher Stowe's anti-slavery novel, *Uncle Tom's Cabin*. Many saw the case as a miscarriage of justice. Green was granted a conditional pardon in March 1862 and told to leave the state within 60 days. He and his wife returned to Talbot County in 1870 and he died there in 1877.

Thomas Garrett continued to work on the Underground Railroad. He died in 1871 of bladder disease. Late in life Garrett wrote: "No labor during a long life has given me so much real happiness as what I have done for the slave." At his funeral, a half-mile-long line of blacks and whites tried to get into the meetinghouse where his funeral service was held. The pallbearers who carried his coffin were all black men.

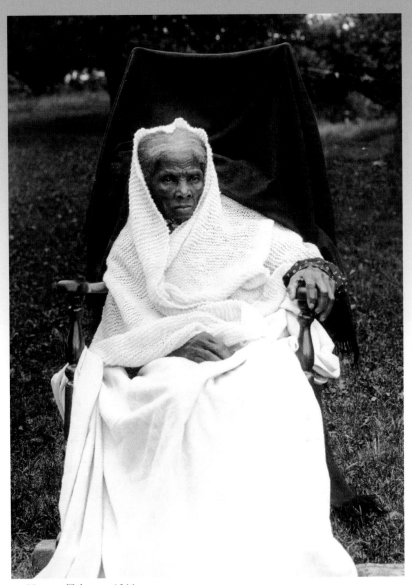

Harriet Tubman, 1911

TIMELINE

C. 1820: Harriet Tubman is born Araminta Ross, a slave, in Bucktown, Dorchester County, Maryland.

1844: Tubman marries John Tubman, a freed black man.

SEPTEMBER 24, 1849: Tubman escapes to the North and changes her first name to Harriet.

1850: The Fugitive Slave Act is passed by Congress and makes it illegal for anyone to aid or abet a runaway slave.

1851: Tubman begins regular trips south to Maryland and Virginia to find slaves seeking freedom and guide them north along the Underground Railroad.

OCTOBER 1856: On a trip to Maryland's Eastern Shore, Tubman escorts a slave named Tilly north and tries, unsuccessfully, to convince her own sister, Rachel, to come north with her.

OCTOBER 29, 1856: Joe Bailey, a slave owned by William Hughlett, resolves to run away after he receives a whipping from his master.

NOVEMBER 8, 1856: Joe, his brother, Bill, and a third slave, Peter Pennington, meet with Tubman to plan their escape from Maryland.

NOVEMBER 15, 1856: The small party of fugitives make their escape.

NOVEMBER 17, 1856: Eliza Manokey, another runaway, joins the group en route to Delaware.

NOVEMBER 18–22, 1856: Tubman's party moves north, staying in safe houses along the way, finally approaching the Christina River Bridge that separates Maryland from Delaware.

NOVEMBER 25, 1856: Tubman and her runaways cross the bridge hidden in two wagons carrying bricks and arrive in Wilmington, Delaware.

NOVEMBER 28, 1856: They arrive in New York City and meet with Underground Railroad agent Oliver Johnson.

December 8, 1856: The fugitives cross the Niagara suspension bridge by train and are finally safe and free in St. Catharines, Ontario, Canada.

1857: Tubman returns to Maryland to bring her parents north to freedom.

November 1860: Tubman make her last journey to Maryland to bring slaves north.

April 1861: The outbreak of the Civil War effectively ends the Underground Railroad.

May 1861–April 1865: During the Civil War, Tubman works as a hospital nurse, spy, and scout for Union raiding parties.

1865: The Thirteen Amendment is ratified, officially ending slavery in the United States.

1908: Tubman opens the John Brown House for Aged and Indigent Negroes in Auburn, New York.

March 10, 1913: Tubman dies in Auburn at about age 92.

2016: Tubman is selected to be the first woman memorialized on U.S. paper money in modern times. Her portrait is scheduled to appear on the $20 bill beginning in 2020.

GLOSSARY

agent (AY-juhnt)—a person who worked to help fugitive slaves on the Underground Railroad

conductor (kuhn-DUHK-tuhr)—a person who helped runaway slaves escape to the North on the Underground Railroad

free state (FREE STAYT)—a state that did not allow slavery in the years before the Civil War

fugitive (FYOO-juh-tiv)—a person fleeing from punishment or intolerable conditions, such as a slave

house slave (HOUSS SLAYV)—a slave who worked in a master's house as a maid, cook, butler, or nursemaid or who performed other domestic chores

Quaker (KWAY-kur)—a member of a religion called the Society of Friends that opposed slavery and violence

ratified (RAT-uh-fide)—formally approved

safe house (SAYF HOUSS)—a place where escaping slaves could hide; people who lived in the houses believed slavery was wrong

slave state (SLAYV STAYT)—a state that allowed slavery in the years before the Civil War

spiritual (SPIHR-it-choo-uhl)—a religious folk song sung originally by black slaves in the South

stationmaster (STAY-shuhn-mass-tuhr)—a leader in organizing and running the Underground Railroad, often in charge of a safe house or series of them

Underground Railroad (UHN-dur-ground RAYL-rohd)—a system of helpful people and safe places for runaway slaves during the mid–1800s

vigilante (vij-uh-LAN-tee)—a person who punishes lawbreakers personally and illegally rather than relying on legal authorities

CRITICAL THINKING USING THE COMMON CORE

1. Some historians say that Harriet Tubman's contribution to the abolition cause went even further than helping some 300 slaves attain their freedom. What reasons do you think they would have for making this statement? Support your answer using information from at least two other texts or valid Internet sources. (Integration of Knowledge and Ideas)

2. The Underground Railroad relied on the support and assistance of a number of people who risked their own welfare to help. Which people helped Tubman and her party on their journey north? What price did some of them pay for working on the Underground Railroad? (Key Ideas and Details)

3. Tubman's experience as related in this book is just one of hundreds of documented rescues along the Underground Railroad in the 1850s. Research another such mission made by Tubman or another conductor on the Underground Railroad using at least two other texts or valid Internet sources. (Integration of Knowledge and Ideas)

INTERNET SITES

FactHound offers a safe, fun way to find Internet sites related to this book. All of the sites on FactHound have been researched by our staff.

Here's all you do:
Visit *www.facthound.com*
Type in this code: 9781515736042

FactHound will fetch the best sites for you!

FURTHER READING

Hale, Nathan. *Underground Abductor*. Nathan Hale's Hazardous Tales. New York: Amulet Books, 2015.

Lassieur, Allison. *The Underground Railroad: An Interactive History Adventure*. You Choose Books. North Mankato, Minn.: Capstone Press, 2016.

McDonough, Yona Zeldis. *What Was the Underground Railroad?* What Was. . . ? New York: Grosset & Dunlap, an imprint of Penguin Group, 2013.

Nolen, Jerdine. *Eliza's Freedom Road: An Underground Railroad Diary*. New York: Simon & Schuster Books for Young Readers, 2011.

SELECTED BIBLIOGRAPHY

Buckmaster, Henrietta. *Let My People Go: The Story of the Underground Railroad and the Growth of the Abolition Movement.* Columbia, S.C.: University of South Carolina Press, published in cooperation with the Institute for Southern Studies and the South Caroliniana Society of the University of South Carolina, 1992.

Clinton, Catherine. *Harriet Tubman: The Road to Freedom.* Boston: Little, Brown, 2004.

Foner, Eric. *Gateway to Freedom: The Hidden History of the Underground Railroad.* New York: W. W. Norton & Company, 2015.

Huimez, Jean M. *Harriet Tubman: The Life and the Life Stories.* Madison: University of Wisconsin Press, 2003.

Lowry, Beverly. *Harriet Tubman: Imagining a Life.* New York: Doubleday, 2007.

INDEX

Bailey, Joe, 9–11, 19–20, 26–28, 30, 33–36, 38–40, 42–43, 45, 54, 57, 61, 65–66, 76–77, 84, 87–90, 93–94, 96–98, 102–103

Bailey, William, 10–11, 20, 30, 38–40, 42, 45–46, 46, 49, 61, 66, 69, 84, 94, 102–103

Garrett, Thomas, 69–72, 83, 104

Green, Reverend, 57–60, 104

Henry, John, 46, 53

Hughlett, William, 9–11, 19–20, 26–28, 30, 33–34, 40, 45, 53–54, 57, 61–62, 65–67, 76–77, 96, 103

Jamestown, Virginia, 4

Manokey, Eliza, 17–18, 46–47, 49–50, 57, 69, 75–76, 84, 93–94, 103

Moses, 97

Niagara Falls, 89, 90, 93

Pennington, Peter, 41–42, 45, 48, 54–55, 61, 84, 94, 102

St. Catharines, Canada, 89, 97, 102

Tilly, 12–14, 23

Tubman, Harriet, 6, 12–14, 23, 25–26, 41–43, 48–50, 55, 57, 59–60, 62, 65–67, 69–71, 74–76, 81–84, 87–90, 94, 97–98, 100–101, 103
    nickname of, 14, 18, 33–36, 40, 42, 46–49, 54, 69, 76, 82–83, 87, 96–97

Tubman, Rachel, 23, 25–26, 103

Underground Railroad, 5, 6, 12, 18, 36, 47, 57, 69, 87

Wilmington, Delaware, 23, 41, 49, 53, 61, 67, 69, 70, 71, 72, 75, 77, 82, 83, 84

Wright, Turpin, 45–46, 53–54

ABOUT THE AUTHOR

Steven Otfinoski has written more than 180 books for young readers. His previous titles in the Tangled History series are about the sinking of the *Titanic*, the Japanese attack on Pearl Harbor, and the John F. Kennedy assassination. Three of his books have been named Books for the Teen Age by the New York Public Library. He lives in Connecticut with his family.